1. Nineteenth-century hair jewellery. (Photograph by Graham Trott.)

The Shire Book

Sentimental Jewellery

Ann Louise Luthi

Printed in Great Britain by CIT Printing
Services, Press Buildings, Merlins Bridge,
Haverfordwest, Pembrokeshire SA61 1XF.

British Library Cataloguing in Publication Data:
Luthi, Ann Louise
Sentimental jewellery. - (The Shire book)
1. Jewelry - History - 18th century 2. Jewelry -
History -19th century 3. Sentimentalism in art
I. Title
391.7'09033
ISBN 0 7478 0363 3

*Published in 1998 by Shire Publications Ltd,
Cromwell House, Church Street, Princes Risborough,
Buckinghamshire HP27 9AA, UK.
Copyright © 1998 by Ann Louise Luthi.
First published 1998. ISBN 0 7478 0363 3.
Ann Louise Luthi is hereby identified as the author of
this work in accordance with Section 77 of the
Copyright, Designs and Patents Act 1988.*
*All rights reserved. No part of this publication may be
reproduced or transmitted in any form or by any
means, electronic or mechanical, including photocopy,
recording, or any information storage and retrieval
system, without permission in writing from the
publishers.*

COVER: *Georgian and early Victorian sentimental brooches.*

ACKNOWLEDGEMENTS

All the jewellery illustrated, unless otherwise indicated, comes from dealers or from private
collections and has been found at antique markets or fairs. I am very grateful to everyone who
has allowed me to photograph their pieces, especially Charlotte Sayers FGA, who read my
text and made some very helpful suggestions.
Most of the photographs were specially taken by Alice Fowler, except for plate 1, which is
by Graham Trott, and the pictures of jet, French jet, vulcanite, bog-oak and horn (plates 35,
36, 37, 38, 40, 53, 60 and 61), which were supplied by Allison Massey. Plate 2 is reproduced
by kind permission of Avril Lansdell; plate 3 by kind permission of the V & A Picture
Library; plate 71 by kind permission of the Ashmolean Museum; and the pictures of the
Birmingham jewellery trade (plates 52, 54, 55, 56 and 57) come from the Jewellery Quarter
Discovery Centre. Plates 46 and 47 are taken by kind permission of Lacis Publications from
The Art of Hair Work by Mark Campbell (Lacis Publications, Berkeley, California, USA;
1989, reprinted 1996).

2. A carte-de-visite of the 1880s shows a young woman wearing crape. She is in the first stage of mourning. Her necklace, brooch and earrings are of carved Whitby jet. (Avril Lansdell.)

CONTENTS

INTRODUCTION

The reasons for wearing jewellery are more complicated than a basic desire for self-adornment. People have used charms and amulets from the earliest times to try to protect themselves against the vast and incomprehensible range of ills that might befall them. In the middle ages there was a belief that certain stones had magical powers: the toadstone was thought to detect poison, the sapphire cured diseases of the skin and the topaz not only cured madness but increased prudence and wisdom as well. Holy relics were also supposed to protect the wearer; they were set in jewels and worn on the person. With so many reminders of the imminence of death and the hazards of life, it is not surprising that *memento mori* (meaning 'Remember that you must die') jewellery should have appeared in the sixteenth century. Memento mori pieces were decorated with skeletons, coffins, skulls, worms and crossbones, all of which seem very macabre to us today.

By the seventeenth century these same symbols were beginning to be used for jewellery which was made not to warn of mortality in general but to commemorate the death of specific individuals. The rapid growth of this custom is generally attributed to the execution of King Charles I in 1649, which inspired his loyal royalist followers to wear jewellery in his memory. His miniature portrait was set in the bezels of rings, sometimes worn secretly, and locks of his hair were much treasured.

In the second half of the seventeenth century the custom began

3. Mourning and memento mori rings of the seventeenth century. (Back row) A miniature of Charles I framed by diamonds, and a ring for Charles II and Catherine of Braganza with a gold-wire crown and initials over woven hair. (Front row) Three memento mori gold rings decorated with enamelled skulls and crossbones. (V & A Picture Library.)

of providing memorial rings for distribution to friends and family after a funeral. In his diaries Samuel Pepys tells of receiving several such gifts, and at his own death in 1703 he left 123 rings to be handed out in his memory. Stuart memorial rings, pendants, lockets and slides (worn on ribbons around the neck or

Above. 4. A Stuart mourning ring with a diamond-shaped rock-crystal bezel over a gold-wire cipher which is set on hair and pink foil. The underside of the bezel has black and white enamel decoration.

5. Three late seventeenth-century memorial pieces. (Centre) A skull and crossbones on hair under faceted crystal, now a stickpin but probably originally a button. (Left and right) A pair of clasps with beaded edges and faceted crystal over gold-wire ciphers, hair and blue silk backgrounds.

Left. 6. Three slides. (Left) A coronet above a gold-wire cipher with two angels set on hair and silk under faceted crystal. (Right) A gold-wire cipher on hair under crystal. (Below) This third slide is upside down to show the loops through which a ribbon could be threaded and an inscription 'My Father & my Husband'.

Right. 7. Three small heart pendants. (Left) A tiny eighteenth-century heart with a scene in hair on one side and hair initials on the back. (Centre) A crown and gold-wire cipher over hair and blue silk. (Right) A double-sided faceted crystal heart with gold-wire ciphers over hair on both sides.

8. Two gold rings with messages. (Left) A seventeenth-century posy ring with an inscription inside the shank, 'Remember thy friend'. (Charlotte Sayers.) (Right) An eighteenth-century ring set with a garnet and rose diamonds and with an inscription on the outside of the shank, 'En perdant j'ai gagné' ('In losing I have gained'). (Lowther Antiques.)

wrist) had backgrounds of silk or plaited hair with a skull and crossbones or other symbols of death under heavily faceted rock crystal. Sometimes the crystal concealed a cipher (initials) with gold-wire decoration, or the bezel itself was shaped as a skull or a coffin. Plain gold bands were enamelled in black on the outside with skeletons and other emblems of death. Any inscription was on the inside. Gold was often decorated with dog-tooth edging and many rings were delicately enamelled on the back of the bezel. These pieces can still occasionally be found, but they are not cheap.

Rings were also often given as love tokens. Posy rings (the name derives from 'poesy', meaning poetry), which had their origins in the middle ages, were simple gold hoops engraved with messages of love in French, the international language of courtship. By the seventeenth century they had become plain on the outside with the loving inscription on the inside. They were usually worn as engagement or wedding rings and, although the posy ring itself went out of fashion in the eighteenth century, it is from these charming and naive early rings that our modern wedding hoops have developed.

Morbid symbols of death continued to be used in English jewellery until well into the eighteenth century, but by 1730 a more light-hearted rococo style had been introduced from France. Mourning rings still had faceted rock-crystal bezels, now with ribbed gold backs, but the shanks were divided into small scrolls with the inscription in raised gold letters on the outside, which was enamelled. Black enamel was widely used but white enamel was introduced at this time for children and unmarried adults. Many rings had no bezel, only a slim, delicately scrolled hoop which was rounded on the inside.

Scrolled gold and enamel ribbons were also used to frame sentimental heart-shaped pendants with a double-sided crystal compartment for a hair curl or, alternatively, an urn painted in sepia. Sometimes these pendants had a bow at the top and were set with tiny pale garnets; messages of love were often in French. Sentiment was now expressed in a more romantic, allegorical style, with motifs like Cupid's bow and arrows, flaming torches of love, turtle doves and entwined hearts. In mourning jewels, gruesome skulls gave way to neo-classical miniature scenes painted in sepia on ivory. The bezel became larger as a result and changed shape. Rings, clasps, brooches and pendants were now made in a marquise,

9. Four eighteenth-century scrolled enamelled mourning rings, three with rock-crystal bezels. Inscriptions on the outside.

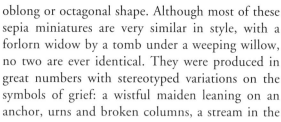

oblong or octagonal shape. Although most of these sepia miniatures are very similar in style, with a forlorn widow by a tomb under a weeping willow, no two are ever identical. They were produced in great numbers with stereotyped variations on the symbols of grief: a wistful maiden leaning on an anchor, urns and broken columns, a stream in the

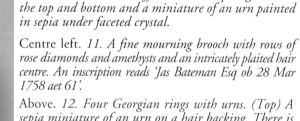

Top left. *10. A mid-eighteenth-century heart-shaped pendant with a white enamel ribbon-scrolled frame inscribed 'Un seul me suffit'. There are pale garnets at the top and bottom and a miniature of an urn painted in sepia under faceted crystal.*

Centre left. *11. A fine mourning brooch with rows of rose diamonds and amethysts and an intricately plaited hair centre. An inscription reads 'Jas Bateman Esq ob 28 Mar 1758 aet 61'.*

Above. *12. Four Georgian rings with urns. (Top) A sepia miniature of an urn on a hair backing. There is an inscription in enamel on the bezel for Ann Nash and on the shank for her husband William. (Left) A gold and black enamel ring with an urn and a serpent in chased gold with a tiny ruby eye. (Right) A white enamel bezel with an urn in black and a compartment for hair. The shank is stranded. (Below) An urn-shaped bezel which has rose diamonds set in silver with black enamel.*

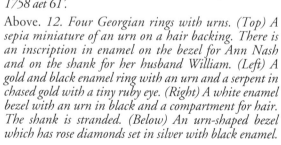

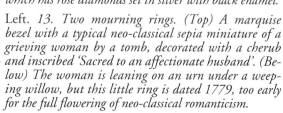

Left. *13. Two mourning rings. (Top) A marquise bezel with a typical neo-classical sepia miniature of a grieving woman by a tomb, decorated with a cherub and inscribed 'Sacred to an affectionate husband'. (Below) The woman is leaning on an urn under a weeping willow, but this little ring is dated 1779, too early for the full flowering of neo-classical romanticism.*

foreground or even a faithful dog. Little snippets of hair were often incorporated into the sepia paint. There was usually a heartbreaking inscription such as 'Not lost but gone before', 'Weep not: it falls to rise again', 'Fate snatched her early to the pitying skies' or 'In death lamented as in life beloved'.

These neo-classical miniatures were not necessarily

Above. *14. A pretty little sentimental Georgian Cupid is painted in the palest colours and bordered by seed pearls.*

15. Two neo-classical rings. (Left) A three-dimensional scene has a classically robed female, two doves and a laurel wreath. The inscription on the back is 'Sacred to friendship'. (Right) More doves, a wreath and another female. (Lowther Antiques.) These are both sentimental rather than memorial pieces.

Below. *16. Two neo-classical mourning pendants. (Left) The grieving woman leans on an anchor by a tomb. Her husband was probably lost at sea. (Right) An unusual variation on the typical scene of mourning: a ship is shown foundering and in the foreground is a dinghy with two small beseeching figures, one with his hands clasped together, the other with arms outstretched. The inscription is for a father and son who died on the same day. This can also be worn as a brooch.*

Above. *17. This portrait medallion of a fashionable Georgian gentleman would have been worn for purely sentimental reasons. His hair and monogram are under glass on the back.*

all memorial pieces. Some were probably given as pledges of love and fidelity. In this case the colours were brighter and the symbols were more cheerful; the maidens, in classical white dresses, were not noticeably grief-stricken; there might be an altar rather than a tomb, and turtle doves, cupids and cherubs hovered overhead. 'Sacred to friendship' was an ambiguous inscription which could be used for either sentiment or sorrow.

It was very fashionable to wear portrait medallions as jewellery at the end of the eighteenth century and into the first two decades of the nineteenth century. They were worn as pendants on long chains or mounted as bracelet clasps. Silhouettes, which were cheaper, were also used in jewellery; they were set in rings or brooches, sometimes with a locket fitting for hair on the back. These too were used for mourning jewellery or as love tokens.

A curious variation on the miniature was a single eye painted in delicate colours, often with an eyebrow and a wispy curl of hair. The most poignant were painted with a small glistening teardrop. An eye had the advantage of mystery and anonymity; it is said that the Prince of Wales (later George IV) gave a locket with a miniature of his right eye to his morganatic wife Mrs Maria Fitzherbert. Although they were later parted, it was a love that endured. When he died in 1830 he was found to be wearing a locket set with Mrs Fitzherbert's portrait around his neck.

As the craze for neo-classicism faded ring bezels became smaller and rounder. Shanks were often made of gold strands, joined at the back and spreading out where they joined the bezel. Plaited

18. Silhouettes were cheaper than painted miniatures. The brooch on the right has an inscription for Henry Butterfield, who died in 1781 aged forty-four.

19. Three painted eyes. The top eye has an eyebrow; the eye on the left has an eyebrow, a hair curl and a border of seed pearls symbolising tears; but the eye on the right has a real diamond tear. (Eye with diamond: Peter Hess.)

20. A Georgian swivel ring. This side has pearls and plaited fair hair.

21. The same ring with the bezel reversed. The black enamel side has an inscription for C. A. Bowerbank, who died in 1815 aged nine.

hair under crystal was still popular for bezels, often bordered with pearls, which signified tears. Inscriptions were now usually on the back of the bezel, though some bezels were made to swivel, showing either hair on one side or an inscription on enamel on the other. Serpents, symbolising eternity, were introduced as a motif, with cross-hatched golden scales and tiny ruby eyes. They were found around the bezels of rings, as the shanks of rings and on the rims of brooches. Padlocks, too, were immensely popular and were found on all kinds of jewellery. Hearts continued in fashion. Small brooches, known as pins, are very typical of late Georgian jewellery. They were usually oblong with a glass compartment for hair (though there was not always hair inside) and a border of chased gold, pearls, garnets, French jet or paste. The most unusual are those shaped as teardrops or as fallen leaves, shells or swans.

The old superstitions about the magic properties of gems were revived when the language of stones became a great passion of the

22. Georgian symbolism. (Left) A padlock with seed pearls and hair. (Right) A textured gold heart set with a turquoise flower and with padlock and key drops. (Charlotte Sayers.)

23. The language of stones. (Top) A mandoline set with gems that spell out REGARD. (Charlotte Sayers.) (Left) A REGARD ring. (Right) A DEAREST ring. (Below) A clasp spelling REGARD in paste. (Rings and clasp: Lowther Antiques.)

early nineteenth century, both in England and in France. Sentimental messages were spelled out by the initial letters of precious or semi-precious stones. 'Regard' was represented by ruby, emerald, garnet, amethyst, ruby and diamond; 'Love' by lapis-lazuli, opal, vermeil (an old name for hessonite garnet) and emerald. 'Dearest' used diamond, emerald, amethyst, ruby, emerald, sapphire and topaz. Turquoises were often set as forget-me-nots with ruby centres, another favourite expression of love. This sentimental use of stones coincided with a new kind of decoration known as 'cannetille' in which the gold was very skilfully worked into a filigree based on embroidery with curls and tiny granules. Some of the prettiest brooches, lockets and rings date from this time. They are very much collected. In contrast, plain simple gold bands were in favour as wedding rings, worn with a jewelled or enamelled keeper ring.

VICTORIAN SENTIMENTAL JEWELLERY

Above. *24. Small early nineteenth-century brooches with hair centres and frames of French jet, paste, pearls, garnets, amethysts and turquoises. The tiny brooch bottom right is a comet made to celebrate the return of Halley's Comet in 1834.*

25. A magnificent pavé-set turquoise serpent with cabochon ruby eyes twined around a turquoise flower with a diamond centre. (Charlotte Sayers.)

There was no immediate change in jewellery styles when Victoria came to the throne in 1837. Although dress and hair styles changed rapidly in the nineteenth century and it is often possible to date a costume to a particular year, jewellery did not change with the same rapidity. Sometimes it is possible to say when a particular jewellery design was first fashionable but it is far more difficult to decide when it finally went out of favour.

The early years of Victoria's reign coincided with the full flowering of the Romantic movement, and no one was more romantic, nor more passionate, than the new Queen. Nature provided the inspiration for jewellers at this time; leaves, buds, flowers, twigs, bunches of grapes and serpents twined freely and charmingly over bracelets, earrings and brooches. The Queen wore a serpent brace-

let at her first Council meeting, and her betrothal ring was a gold serpent studded with emeralds. Serpent rings were seldom out of fashion throughout the nineteenth century. When the serpent's tail was in its mouth it symbolised eter-

26. *A selection of hands. (Centre) A gold bracelet with a hand clasp which has a turquoise flower cuff of its own. (Charlotte Sayers.) The hair choker has a hand clasp which is meant to be worn at the front. (Bottom left) A gold hand grasping a serpent. (Right) A hand carved from lava with a gold bracelet, coral and a ring. (Last two hands: Lowther Antiques.)*

nity. Turquoise, coral, ivory and seed pearls were still popular. A single hand, offering love or friendship, was often carved from coral or ivory in the early years of Victoria's reign and was a common motif of later jet or vulcanite brooches. Hands were also used for clasps on gold or pinchbeck chains. Gold, which was chased, pierced or engraved, was the most generally used material although pinchbeck, an alloy of copper and zinc invented by the eighteenth-century watchmaker Christopher Pinchbeck, was often used for less expensive jewellery. Gilt jewellery was usually mercury-gilt. The bracelet was the most popular type of jewellery, and gold or

Below left. *27. Three mourning rings which are fully hallmarked. (Top left) A wide hoop with black enamel, inscribed 'In Memory Of' and with hallmarks for 1838. (Top right) A wide gold hoop with 'In Memory Of' in black enamel; hallmarks for 1841. (Sam Asprey.) (Below) A narrow band inscribed inside for Peter Cullen, who died aged ninety-four, a great age in 1833.*

Below right. *28. Victorian brooches with multiple hair arrangements. These were not mourning brooches commemorating a family disaster but sentimental tokens to celebrate a special event. The butterfly brooch has the hair of nine members of one family, only two of whom had died. The flower brooch is for ten people named on the back, and the brooch of aquamarine paste is for four boys and two girls, probably a present for their grandmother.*

29. Mourning brooches were beginning to change by the 1840s and 1850s. 'In Memory Of' is unusual in blue enamel. (Black enamel brooch on left: Charlotte Sayers.)

gilt bracelets were worn constantly, often in pairs.

Many mourning rings were now gold hoops with a chased rim ornamented by black enamel and with an inscription on the outside of the band. Unlike gem-set rings, they had to be hallmarked, as tax was payable. Cannetille was seldom seen after about 1840. The pretty little brooches that were so common in the early years of the nineteenth century continued to be popular, but, unless jet or black enamel is used or there is a personal inscription on the back or 'In Memory Of' on the front, it cannot be assumed that these are always mourning pieces. They are frequently sentimental. By mid-century brooches had become larger, black enamel was used extensively, the frames were scrolled, and hair arrangements were becoming ever more elaborate. Gothic Revival jewellery, with its emphasis on medieval crosses and quatrefoils, was taken up by English designers like the architect Augustus Pugin.

Changes came about as the middle classes became more socially confident and increasingly prosperous. Independent young women studied geology, botany and zoology. In 1851 the Great Exhibition in the Crystal Palace provided a marvellous opportunity for innovation and manufacture. Science, art and archaeology provided the inspiration for design. Novelty was all-important. The jewellery trade thrived, while the discovery of gold in California in 1849 and in Australia in 1851 gave it a great impetus.

By 1860 jewellery was no longer romantic, imaginative and delicate but had become much larger and bolder, greatly influenced by the discovery of Etruscan, Greek and Egyptian jewellery. This is the period which produced jewellery in the style now thought of as typically 'Victorian'.

Then came the event that was responsible for the greatest changes of all. 1861 was a very bad year for Queen Victoria. In March her mother, the Duchess of Kent, died. Devastated though she was by her grief, the Queen was nevertheless able to order the customary jewels to commemorate her mother. Lockets, brooches, bracelets and

30. A gold locket in Gothic Revival style. It has plaited hair inside.

15

31. Men also wore sentimental jewellery. The turquoise stickpin opens to reveal a hair arrangement and the marquise-shaped one has two hearts on an altar with a dove bearing a laurel wreath. The three Order of the Garter studs were made specially by Garrards, the Crown Jewellers. They have dyed hair decorations under glass.

pins were soon distributed in her memory. But worse was to follow. In November Prince Albert was taken ill and three weeks later he unexpectedly died. He was only forty-two. The Queen, who was the same age, was inconsolable and plunged herself into deepest mourning for the rest of her life.

She was not alone. The rules of mourning were strict and complex, while the number of relatives for whom mourning was necessary was extensive. Even connections by marriage were commemorated as if they had been members of the family. The high mortality rate of the time, especially of infants, meant that some women could spend many years of their lives in mourning. Indeed it has been suggested that many elderly women continued, out of habit, to wear black bombazine and crape even when they were not officially obliged to do so.

Queen Victoria in the seclusion of her widowhood at Windsor set an example to the rest of Britain. Even before Albert died she had dutifully observed the rituals of death and mourning. Not only was black to be worn by her subjects but the jewellery which was allowable was strictly limited. Jet was the most favoured material at court, but onyx and black enamel were equally acceptable. Hair, cut-steel, Berlin ironwork, ivory and tortoiseshell were amongst the materials which could be worn in the later stages of mourning.

32. A fashion plate from about 1855 shows bracelets worn on both wrists. Three have been coloured to look like hair.

The Queen's intense misery soon found an outlet in commissioning jewellery to give in memory of her beloved husband. Garrards, the Crown Jewellers, started work a few days after his death. For years afterwards a steady stream of commemorative jewellery was lovingly distributed by Victoria to her increasingly large family.

It was not just the members of the Royal Family or the Court who wore mourning jewellery. Society was changing rapidly, and

33. The standardised message 'In Memory Of' in black enamel round the bezel of a ring became common in the mid nineteenth century.

Left. 34. Other mourning pieces with black enamel and 'In Memory Of'. The superior pendant on the right says 'In Memory Of A Beloved Son'. (Lowther Antiques.)

35. Jet bracelets with typical Victorian symbols. (Left) A padlock. (Right) An anchor (hope), a heart (charity) and a cross (faith). (Allison Massey.)

the demand for comparatively inexpensive jewellery was growing. The poignant personal inscriptions and the delicacy of the mourning jewellery of the early years of the century gave way to larger, more sombre jewels. The jet industry in Whitby flourished and the Hallmarking Act of 1854 allowed lower-grade gold alloys to be used, whilst mass-production methods resulted in cheaper brooches and lockets, many of them in black enamel with the impersonal standardised lettering 'In Memory Of'. It is not difficult to identify a piece of this later Victorian mourning jewellery. It is usually large, well-made, typical of its age and ponderous, and a lot of it has survived.

Although the wearing of mourning jewellery was widespread, other sentimental jewellery continued to be made. Wedding rings were now plain wide gold bands, while pearls and diamonds were considered most suitable for engagement rings. Necklaces invariably had something dangling from them. Usually these were lockets of jet or gold, but pendants and crosses were also popular. When a piece of jewellery combines a cross with an anchor and a heart, these symbolise faith, hope and charity. Flowers (especially the forget-me-not), butterflies, insects, bees, horseshoes, shells, buckles and stars were all favourite motifs. Serpents were still in fashion.

JET, HAIR AND OTHER UNUSUAL MATERIALS

Although the Romans made jewellery from the jet they found when they invaded Britain, there was no organised jet industry from the time that they left until the beginning of the nineteenth century. Jet is a form of coal that is light in weight and an intense black colour. It can be carved or drilled and will take a very high polish. The finest jet is found at Whitby in North Yorkshire in seams that occur not only in the local cliffs but also extend under the sea. Jet was usually found washed up on the beach, but as demand grew other methods of obtaining it became necessary and from about 1840 it was mined.

The industry was revived in the early years of the nineteenth century when a method of turning jet beads was discovered. In 1825 there were two workshops in Whitby and by 1850 there were seven workshops, including that of Thomas Andrews, 'jet ornament maker to HM Queen Victoria'. In the following year jet jewellery was shown with great success at the Great Exhibition. After Prince Albert died in 1861 the demand for jet jewellery increased immensely. The combination of lathe turning with hand-carved detail and standardised designs enabled the industry to turn out large quantities of jet jewellery. Workers became very skilled.

36. A very fine carved Whitby jet necklace with a carved pendent cross. (Allison Massey.)

Right. *37. A bog-oak bracelet and two brooches. The brooch on the far right is a very common bog-oak design. (Allison Massey.)*

19

Above. *38. Hands were always popular symbols in Victorian jewellery. These three late examples are in horn. (Allison Massey.)*

Above. *39. Three generations of one family are commemorated in a mourning ring with plaited hair around the shank. The black enamel is for the grandfather, who died in 1791 aged forty-three. The white enamel is for his son, who died three months later, and the shield and an inscription inside the shank are for his daughter's son, who died in 1794 aged one year and twenty-two days.*

40. Moulded and dyed horn pieces simulating jet. (Allison Massey.)

41. A hair necklace with matching earrings. The earrings are hinged with a 'back fitting' and are not easy to put on without the help of a maid.

Above left. *42. More hair earrings. At the top is a pair made in the shape of acorns. At the bottom is a pair of 'top and drop' earrings made with hair that has been dyed red. Hoop or 'creole' earrings became fashionable in 1850. Hair is very light and comfortable to wear.*

Above right. *43. Hair bracelets were given as tokens of love as early as the seventeenth century. These are all nineteenth-century examples, showing the different ways in which hair could be used. The bracelet with charms is American and made from the hair of five different members of the same family.*

Since jet is very light, bulky pieces of jewellery could be worn without discomfort. Chains, lockets, earrings, brooches and necklaces were all made on a grand scale. Bead necklaces and bracelets were threaded on elastic or cord. Other pieces were wired and glued together.

Inevitably imitations of jet soon came on to the market. The most successful was vulcanite, an early form of hardened rubber or gutta percha which is also known as ebonite. It was black when new, could be moulded into intricate designs and took a good polish. Over the years, however, much vulcanite has faded on exposure to light and now has a brownish tinge. It can usually be distinguished from true jet by its colour and signs of moulding.

French jet is black glass, which looks and feels very different from true jet. It is much colder and has a glittery quality. Large pieces are

44. Hair brooches were very fashionable. Lyres, anchors, bows and crescents were all popular. The little oval brooch has a Cupid cameo. (Cupid: Madeleine Popper.)

21

45. Antoni Forrer of Hanover Street was an 'Artist in Hair and Jewellery. By appointment to the Queen'. These instructions were written inside the lid of one of his bracelet boxes.

often mounted on metal. It can also be made into tiny beads which when set around brooches or rings are almost indistinguishable from real jet.

Bog-oak was not made as an imitation of jet but looks very similar. It was used for mourning and religious pieces, particularly in Ireland. Tortoiseshell and horn, when moulded and dyed, were other natural materials that were used instead of jet. Ivory was sometimes used in combination with jet.

Another unusual material much used in mourning and sentimental jewellery is human hair. As early as the seventeenth century hair bracelets were worn as tokens of love by both men and women. More frequently, in Stuart times, hair was used as a background under heavily faceted rock crystal in rings and slides. Hair continued in use throughout the eighteenth century, worn as bracelets, or under glass in almost every piece of sentimental jewellery. In the early nineteenth century jewellers started using hair as a material in its own right. It was woven and plaited in a manner very similar to lacemaking and was then mounted with gold or gilt fittings. Antoni Forrer, who was hairworker by ap-

46. Mark Campbell's book 'Self-Instructor in the Art of Hair-Work' was published in the United States in 1875. This illustration from the book shows its author seated at a braiding table.

47. Examples of hairwork pictures offered for sale by Mark Campbell in the 'catalog of hair jewellery' which was included in his book 'Self-Instructor in the Art of Hair-Work'.

23

Left. *48. Horsehair was also used for jewellery, but it was coarser than human hair and the designs are more limited. Chain links and coiled disks are typical. It was sometimes dyed red.*

Above. *49. A handsome early nineteenth-century Berlin iron necklace which was cast and then lacquered black. (Madeleine Popper.)*

pointment to Queen Victoria, and Lemmonier et Cie of Paris were the most fashionable of the many makers of hair jewellery. They both won Prize Medals at the Great Exhibition. Lemmonier prided himself on the fine quality of his work and embellished his pieces with turquoises and gems.

Hair arrangements under glass continued to be popular and increasingly elaborate: Prince of Wales feathers, flower bouquets and even cornucopias were favourite subjects. There was, however, always a suspicion that unscrupulous jewellers substituted the hair of strangers for that of the beloved.

An enterprising lady called Alexanna Speight produced a book for amateurs called *The Lock of Hair* which gave detailed instructions in the making of hair devices. At the same time in the United States of America Mark Campbell published a book with directions for plaiting hair. They both also sold the kits that were necessary for this do-it-yourself work.

50. Another type of iron jewellery, which is thought to have come from Silesia in the late eighteenth century, was made of very fine strands of wire woven into a mesh. This Silesian bracelet is a good example. (Madeleine Popper.)

Left. 51. Cut-steel butterflies from the middle of the nineteenth century are shown beside a much earlier mesh steel bracelet with cut-steel paillettes and butterflies. (Madeleine Popper.)

Other unusual materials that were permissible within the mourning code were Berlin ironwork and cut-steel. Berlin ironwork, which was cast and lacquered black, was first made for patriotic Prussian women who exchanged gold jewellery for iron to help their country in the war against France. Iron wedding rings, proudly inscribed '*Gold gab ich für Eisen*' ('I gave gold for iron'), became status symbols in 1813. Great artistry and skill went into the making. Berlin ironwork is now quite scarce.

Cut-steel was seldom made primarily as mourning jewellery, but it was much used in the later stages of mourning, especially in France. Pieces in good condition are hard to find as it is prone to rust and very difficult to clean.

52. Advertisement for Smith & Pepper, who were manufacturing jewellers in Birmingham from the end of the nineteenth century until 1981. The original factory is now a museum. (Jewellery Quarter Discovery Centre.)

SMITH & PEPPER
77 & 78, VYSE STREET, BIRMINGHAM
Bracelets, Brooches, Pendants, Necklets, Earrings, Crosses, Etc., Etc.
Specialities : BAMBOO, NELLIE STEWART & SLAVE BANGLES

S&P TRADE MARK.

MANUFACTURING JEWELLERS
INDENTS THROUGH MERCHANTS

THE END OF THE NINETEENTH CENTURY

Although photographs had already begun to take the place of painted miniatures by the middle of the nineteenth century, it was not until the invention of the dry plate in the 1880s, and especially the introduction of the Eastman Kodak camera in 1888, that photographs became small enough to use in jewellery. Soon these new, much cheaper portraits were mounted in brooches and lockets, which increased in size to display them. Typical brooches at this time had a photograph under glass on one side and plaited hair on the back. Often they were made to swivel on a heavy gold or gilt frame. It is usually comparatively easy to tell the difference between compartments meant for hair, which were sealed, and those for photographs, which were hinged and made to be opened.

53. Four pieces of Whitby jet. The locket at the bottom has a silver paste cross on the front and hair and a photograph inside. The locket above left has the monogram AEI, meaning 'forever' or 'amity, eternity and infinity', on the front. (Allison Massey.)

54. A photograph from 1897 showing a jewellery workshop in Birmingham. This is entitled 'Making cheap brooches'. (Jewellery Quarter Discovery Centre.)

55. A jewellery workshop in Birmingham in 1897, showing men engraving and embossing. (Jewellery Quarter Discovery Centre.)

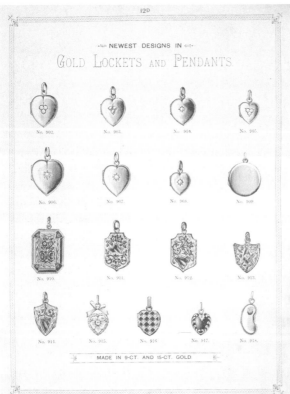

Above. 56. *Women working in a Birmingham workshop in 1897. They are carding and boxing cheap jewellery. (Jewellery Quarter Discovery Centre.)*

57. *A page from an early Smith & Pepper catalogue. (Jewellery Quarter Discovery Centre.)*

58. Mourning brooches in the second half of the nineteenth century became larger, blacker and heavier. Here are two with forget-me-nots; the rest have hair. (Sam Asprey, Jean Archer, Deidre Soames.)

59. A photograph of the whole family is on the back of this silver brooch. The front is illustrated in plate 62. (Peter Hess.)

These photographic mementoes were not only used for mourning jewels but were also frequently of living relatives, friends and sweethearts.

By 1885, after more than twenty years of heavy mourning, the public in general, and the jewellery trade in particular, were becoming thoroughly tired of mourning jewellery in dark sombre colours and longed for a change. An approach was made to the Princess of Wales asking for her help. It was two years before there was a reply. At last, in 1887, the year of Queen Victoria's State Jubilee, there was a relaxation of the rules and the Queen agreed to wear a few pieces of silver jewellery on special occasions. Finally the long years of strict mourning were over. In Whitby the boom in jet was already coming to an end; by 1884 there were fewer than three hundred workers left in the industry. Hair jewellery was now regarded as being in the worst possible taste. In Birming-

60. The bracelet and necklace are French jet; the big brooch is Whitby jet. The two 'In Memory Of' brooches for 'My Dear Mother' on the left and 'My Dear Father' on the right were mass-produced in cheap metal frames. (Allison Massey.)

ham the silver trade began to plan for expansion and the Birming-ham Jewellers' and Silversmiths' Association was formed. One of its first moves was to provide training in artistic design for young people at the Municipal School of Art.

Silver jewellery was high fashion during the 1870s and 1880s, especially large oval lockets with bulky chains, and there was a craze for western interpretations of Japanese styles. The public, however, was fickle, and by 1890 silver was again out of favour with fashionable society. The discovery of the Comstock Lode in Nevada, USA, enormously increased the world's supply of silver,

61. The Diamond Jubilee of Queen Victoria in 1897 was marked by the production of commemorative pieces like these two in vulcanite. (Allison Massey.)

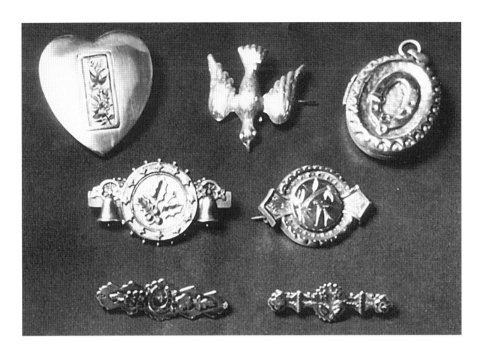

62. Silver love jewellery ranged in price from the very inexpensive, like the bar brooches at the bottom and the stamped-out locket with room for photographs inside, to the fine-quality silver heart with an enamelled panel of a bird and flowers. (Jean Archer, Peter Hess, Deidre Soames; heart from Sam Asprey.)

causing a corresponding decrease in price, while tax concessions in 1890 led to the start of a 'trinket trade'. Down the social scale, small pieces of sentimental silver jewellery became immensely popular. Of all the inexpensive items that flooded the market, the silver love brooch was probably the favourite. It could be bought at a price that was within reach of all but the very poor. The manufacture of such pieces was simple. Silver sheet was cut to shape by presses and the decoration was put on with a stamp. If more than one part was involved, the individual pieces were soldered together. Sometimes a little hand engraving was applied or an area was left plain so there was room for a name or decoration to be added according to the wishes of the customer. The edges were often beaded or scalloped.

The variety of the designs was enormous. Many expressed the symbolism so beloved by the Victorians. The 'language of flowers' supplied the inspiration for many of the designs: bluebells meant constancy; forget-me-nots, true love; ivy, friendship, fidelity and marriage; honeysuckle, bonds of love; lilies of the valley, the return of happiness; and rosemary was for remembrance. The language of flowers was the subject of numerous books which provided a guide to the interpretation of all the different flowers.

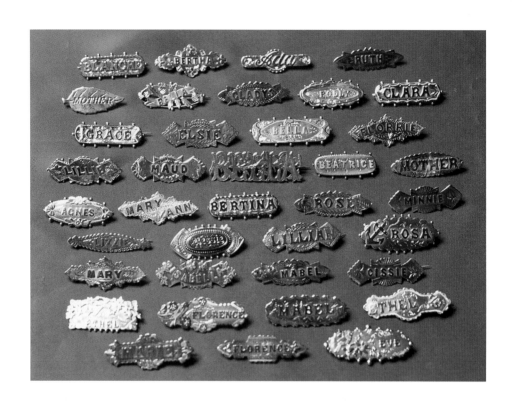

Above. *63. A collection of silver name brooches. (Jean Archer.)*

64. 'Mizpah' (see pages 33-4) and 'Best wishes' brooches in inexpensive gilt metal. (Peter Hess, Jean Archer.)

Left. *65. A gold ring with the names Mother and Father spelled out in diamond chips. (Madeleine Popper.)*

Below. *66. A diamond arrow above, a pearl arrow below; both second half of the nineteenth century. (Sam Asprey, Charlotte Sayers.)*

The prettiest of these love brooches often had touches of rose gold applied to the flowers and yellow gold to the leaves. Symbolism was not restricted to flowers: horseshoes, clasped hands, hearts, lovebirds, harps, buckles and lovers' knots were all common. Many love brooches were produced to commemorate the Queen's Diamond Jubilee. They often have two hearts, as well as 'VR', a crown and the dates 1837-97.

Equally popular were silver name brooches, which can still be found in great numbers. They were often given as presents. Many are for 'Mother' or 'Baby', while others are for the girls' names that were popular in Victorian working-class families. Some names, such as Nellie, Maud, Dora and Ida, are no longer as common now as they were at the end of the nineteenth century, while others, like Alice, Emily, Rose, Lucy and Annie, are still popular today and so are less easy to find. Collecting name brooches is not very expensive and can give much pleasure. Names can also be found carved in jet.

Some love brooches carried messages like 'Best wishes' or 'Merry thoughts'. The commonest type is the 'Mizpah' brooch, which was given when lovers or close relations were about to be parted, often by war. The word comes from the Old Testament (Genesis 31: 49): 'And Mizpah; for he said, The Lord watch between me and thee, when we are absent, one from another.' 'Mizpah' was also used on lockets, bangles or rings, sometimes in gold. Twin hearts signified united love.

At the end of the century tastes and styles were changing again. By the time the Queen died in 1901 there was a revival of late Georgian design, and 'Regard' rings, brooches and pendants were again high fashion. Wedding rings by now were narrow bands of gold. The influence of the Arts and Crafts movement in England and Art Nouveau jewellers like Lalique in France meant not only that new jewellery bore no resemblance to the immediate Victorian past but also that the favourite materials were very different. Jet, hairwork, onyx, black enamel and all forms of mourning jewellery were now viewed with repugnance. In spite of the sinking of the *Titanic* in 1912 and the great loss of life in the First World War, there was to be no revival of mourning jewellery in the twentieth century.

Much antique sentimental jewellery is often described, rather disparagingly, as 'secondary' jewellery. These pieces were not intended to be worn on grand state occasions. The materials from which they were made were not particularly expensive. Gold was used sparingly; gems were often paste or semi-precious stones, and silver brooches could be mass-produced cheaply. Even when diamonds, emeralds and rubies were used, the stones were small; owners and jewellers were not tempted to recycle them in the latest fashion, as they were with much grander, ancestral jewels.

It is still possible to find Georgian and Victorian sentimental jewellery for a reasonable price at antique markets and fairs. The discerning buyer will learn a lot from handling and looking at each piece. Take a 10x lens and look carefully at the back as well as the front. Be wary about buying pieces that have been obviously altered or repaired. Rings frequently have had shanks replaced, and the pins on brooches are prone to break. When in doubt, do not buy. Dealers are usually happy to share their knowledge with someone who is genuinely interested. They enjoy selling to collectors. If you can, pay in cash; credit cards are not popular and you will have to pay more for the privilege.

67. Two different types of loupe, both having a 10x lens.

Most antique jewellery is not hallmarked. Mourning rings without bezels were the only articles of jewellery that were legally required to be hallmarked until 1855, when the Wedding Ring

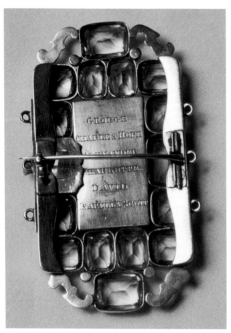

68. Always look at the back. This is a clasp which has been converted to a brooch. The work has been well done but the original rings can still be seen.

Act was passed. A dealer will sometimes test for gold and can tell you if a particular piece is high carat. Many silver love and name brooches are not hallmarked either; often they were made from melted-down coinage, but do not be deterred by the absence of a hallmark from buying something you really like.

Taking care of your jewellery is very important. Jewellery boxes in which the pieces can scratch each other are the cause of much damage. If possible separate each item. Keep rings in ring boxes and take them off when scrubbing the floor or doing the washing up.

69. Vulcanite loses colour when exposed to light. This locket is no longer the glossy black it was originally.

70. A silver buckle ring and a gold 'Mizpah' ring. Both are modern reproductions and should be hallmarked accordingly.

Cleaning jewellery can cause damage too. Gentle cleaning is always best. Warm water with a little detergent is often all that is needed, though you should never immerse anything which is in a closed setting or under glass. Polish silver with a soft impregnated cloth rather than using a harsh chemical cleaner like silver dip. Cotton buds are useful for wiping. If stones are loose or cracked then do not try to clean them yourself. Take them to an expert.

Finally, always take great care when handling your jewellery. It is a good idea to use a soft covering on any table top or work surface. Paper or cloth will do, but a padded surface is best. Your antique jewellery has survived as long as it has because it was cared for by its owners in the past.

FURTHER READING

Becker, Vivienne. *Antique and Twentieth Century Jewellery*. NAG Press, 1980; reprinted 1987.

Bury, Shirley. *Introduction to Rings*. HMSO, 1984.

Bury, Shirley. *Introduction to Sentimental Jewellery*. HMSO, 1984.

Cooper, Diana, and Battershill, Norman. *Victorian Sentimental Jewellery*. David & Charles, 1972.

Dawes, Ginny Redington, and Davidov, Corinne. *Victorian Jewelry – Unexplored Treasures*. Abbeville Press, New York, 1991.

Flower, Margaret. *Victorian Jewellery*. Cassell, 1951.

Muller, Helen. *Jet Jewellery and Ornaments*. Shire, 1980; reprinted 1994.

Munn, Geoffrey C. *The Triumph of Love*. Thames & Hudson, 1993.

Newman, Harold. *An Illustrated Dictionary of Jewelry*. Thames & Hudson, 1981; paperback, 1987.

Phillips, Clare. *Jewelry: From Antiquity to the Present*. Thames & Hudson, 1996 (paperback).

Poynder, Michael. *Price Guide to Jewellery*. Antique Collectors' Club, 1976; revised and reprinted 1990.

PLACES TO VISIT

Before travelling, visitors are advised to find out the opening times and to check that items of interest will be on display.

Ashmolean Museum of Art and Archaeology, Beaumont Street, Oxford OX1 2PH. Telephone: 01865 278000.

British Museum, Great Russell Street, London WC1B 3DG. Telephone: 0171-636 1555.

Fitzwilliam Museum, Trumpington Street, Cambridge CB2 1RB. Telephone: 01223 332900.

Iveagh Bequest, Kenwood House, Hampstead Lane, London NW3 7JR. Telephone: 0181-348 1286.

Jewellery Quarter Discovery Centre, 75-9 Vyse Street, Hockley, Birmingham B18 6HA. Telephone: 0121-554 3598.

Museum of Costume, Assembly Rooms, Bennett Street, Bath, Somerset BA1 2QH. Telephone: 01225 477752.

Museum of London, London Wall, London EC2Y 5HN. Telephone: 0171-600 3699.

Pittville Pump Room Museum, Pittville Park, Cheltenham, Gloucestershire. Telephone: 01242 523852.

Ulster Museum, Botanical Gardens, Belfast, Northern Ireland BT9 5AB. Telephone: 01232 383000.

Victoria and Albert Museum, Cromwell Road, South Kensington, London SW7 2RL. Telephone: 0171-938 8500.

Whitby Museum, Pannett Park, Whitby, North Yorkshire YO21 1RE. Telephone: 01947 602908.

UNITED STATES OF AMERICA

Henry Francis du Pont Winterthur Museum, Route 52, Winterthur, Delaware 19735.

Museum of Mourning Art, Drexel Hill, Pennsylvania.

71. Mourning ring for Queen Anne, who died in 1714. The bezel is coffin-shaped with a crown, initials and a skull and crossbones on a hair background. (Ashmolean Museum.)

INDEX